Because He *Loves* Me

Discovering Our Identity in Christ as
Daughters of the King

By
Deborah Veuger

Because He *Loves* Me

By Deborah Veuger
www.deborahveuger.ca
email: missi1@shaw.ca
Published by Drycreek Publishing
Copyright 2016 by Deborah Veuger
All rights reserved

Cover by ChristianAuthorsGetPaid.com
Photography by Chelsea Bootsman

Printed in Canada

ISBN 978-0-9949490-1-1

For my mom and dad

Because you always loved me

WHAT OTHERS ARE SAYING

Struggling with our sense of identity and value comes out of a deep place of introspection. We've all been there. Out of her own journey, Deborah speaks into this struggle in ways that warm our hearts and bring about a new sense of significance and healing. Her compassion and wise insight show through on each page. Enjoy the journey as she unfolds the powerful story of a Heavenly Father who waits to shower love and grace on us today- because He loves us!

Pastor Verna Verity, *Connecting Ministries-Crossroads Church*

Over the many years I've had the privilege to journey alongside of Deborah observing her life unfold and span into a beautiful array of warm and vibrant colors. She has experienced both the joys and heartaches that come with life's relationships yet has emerged with the Father's heart...reflecting His light, love and forgiveness. Debbie truly is the Heavenly Father's special workmanship and humbly lives as the daughter of the King. She runs to Him daily to be replenished with love and then pours that bountiful supply out to all who come in contact with her. She knows her identity in the King and will draw out of you the song in your heart, then she'll beautifully sing it to you when you have forgotten the words. Get ready to become all that the King has destined you to be! "My heart is stirred by a noble theme as I recite my verses for the King, my tongue is the pen of a skillful writer." Psalm 45:1

You are loved with an overflowing measure from the Heavenly Father...always.

Marcia Lee, *Lifelong friend*

This study gives hope, assurance and offers freedom to all women who have experienced and suffered from the effects of an absentee father or possibly at the hands of someone who was physically or sexually abusive to them. The writer shares: "God has equipped us for everything He wants us to do;" and uses scripture such as 1 Peter 2:9-10 to encourage us that we are Daughters of the King and that we can be free of shame, guilt and can walk in God's marvelous light.

We as women can gain great insight and understanding of our own behaviors and responses to men and ultimately our Lord and Savior by confronting our past through the scriptures and through insights of this study.

By going through these teachings step by step we begin to realize that we do not have to carry guilt or shame from our past or feel unworthy of God's complete forgiveness. We do not need to live our life continually seeking acceptance by God, because of our past pain and issues. We are daughters of the King and God completely accepts us. We are redeemed and forgiven when we come to Him with our hurts and our pain.

The writer helps us reflect through scripture and ultimately helps us find a path to asking the Father to renew our mind and take every thought captive so that we can walk as His Daughters.

I would recommend this study to all women who are looking for a renewed experience with God as being their Father and to all those who want to minister to others who have been hurt or abused in their body and spirit.

Patti Brady, Deputy Executive Director, Bent Arrow Healing Society, Life Long Friend

In the years I have known Deborah, I have seen this book lived out in her daily walk with Jesus. She believes what she says - our best identity is one found in the person of Jesus Christ. May this book inspire you to dig deeper and find out what Debra already has - that there is great life found in Jesus and that His character is yours to have.

Reverend Dallas Lundell, Pastor of Worship Arts,
Crossroads Church

Deborah Veuger

ACKNOWLEDGEMENTS

There are so many people that I would like to thank who have encouraged me and supported me in the efforts to write and create this devotional for women who like me, are longing not only to hear the voice of the King, but desire a deeper understanding of His love and acceptance for us.

First, to women who let me "practise" this devotional with them, week after week, while watching to see what God would do in each of our lives. You were truly gracious and loving as we experienced Jesus moving in our groups and in each other. I will always be grateful for each of you.

Thank you my friend, Kim Cochraine, for introducing me to Kathleen Mailer who encouraged me not only to prefect the devotional but to publish it as well. You both are truly a blessing and gift in my life. Ruth Yesmaniski, my editor, for your constant encouragement and support. I could not have done this without your expertise, wisdom, patience and grace. You have become a true friend and I'm so thankful for you.

To my dear friends, Patti Bradi, Marcia Lee, Verna Verity, Kathy and Dallas Lundell. You have always believed in me. Thank you for your encouragement, spiritual insight and wisdom, love and continuous acceptance of this project.

To my children, Daniel, Christian and Melissa, how I love you and thank Jesus for you in my life. Your love, laughter, hugs and prayers bless me more than you know. Thank you for the grandchildren too, Heidi, Ezekiel, Elijah, Eden, Eva, Eddie and Henry. It takes my breath away how much I love each and every one of them.

To my husband and best friend, Julian. Words cannot describe how grateful I am to you and how much I love you. You have encouraged me through every step of this journey. And I could not have done it without your support and constant belief in me. Thank you that you love Jesus and thank you that you love me. I am blessed.

Most of all, to my Heavenly Father, who I know loves me, accepts me, forgives me lavishly and has plans and purposes just for me. Everyday He shows me that I truly am His daughter and He is my king!........ For now and all eternity.

FOREWORD
By Deborah Veuger

"Who am I?"

These were the words that formulated in her mind and the ones she pondered even though she seemed to be "more than accomplished" evidenced by everything that she had done. To look at her you would say "accomplished", "successful", "career women" and so much more!" By the world's standards she was a success!!

Yet even as a woman of God, deep down inside, she longed for something more, a desire to just be loved... accepted... chosen...and worthy of something or someone. Not to have to strive for one more thing, to feel like she had to have it all together, and to have to be the "best" at all that she laid her hands to do. To not feel the need to be needed...to get over the idea that she was the "only one that could do a good job"... To celebrate someone else's talents without feeling jealous or to constantly compare herself to another... and always in her mind, fall short.

And just for a moment... breathe. She longed for more... more of what would bring her inner peace... and joy. To really know who she was, and to really believe that Jesus loved her and had plans and purposes for just her. To truly believe that she was the daughter of the King, of the most High God who died just for her.

I was that woman longing for something deeper in my walk with Jesus. Wanting to truly believe that my life mattered, scars and all, and to finally **know** I am loved.

One very ordinary day, that all changed. It was the day that I truly discovered what it means to be the Daughter of the King. Come and discover your identity too.

CONTENTS

Deborah Veuger

INTRODUCTION

This is probably one of the most exciting times in history as a woman, with rights and freedoms that many generations have not had the privilege to enjoy. Centuries of history has shown us the oppressions of women in social class, culture and the discrimination of women solely alone based on gender. In the times of Jesus, women in Palestine were subjected to many rejections. They were not counted as having a legitimate voice in the court system, as having a reliable testimony, they were not to be included in the minimum number of ten required for a service to take place in a synagogue and were not considered fit for education. They were often segregated from the rest of society, mostly confined to their homes.

Secularly, some of our esteemed philosophers of ancient Greece, for instance, Aristotle, was said to be far less than sympathetic towards women. He described women as having lack of reason to determine the Good and therefore were obligated to be obedient to achieve virtue (Bar On, p. 145) [1]. He defined women as being the physical opposite to the spiritual male and claimed that women were merely passive receptacles who bore and nurtured the life created by the semen supplied by the spiritual male. (Gould, p. 125) [2] He also shared Plato's notion that women are the opposite of men and connected to the body, but did not adopt his belief that there was potential for growth beyond that state. He described women as "children who never grew up" (Sealey, p.151) [3]. I would love for those two men to have been interviewed by the women of the popular day time show "The View". I'm not sure they would have lasted more than two minutes with the famous female interviewer Barbara Walters in her concise and no nonsense approach, setting the record straight on women's value, rights, and privileges.

Today, in most countries around the world, women have the ability to choose higher forms of education, meaningful careers, financial freedom, hold government and political offices and have a voice and influence in church leadership. Jesus's bold declaration and love for the complete body of Christ, in which He courageously included women in his own personal inner circle of confidants exemplified His endorsement of women throughout the ages and in all nations. He valued them and challenged those prejudices even in the church, which was an anti-women culture of that era. Today women are Pastors and teachers, in addition to having church board and eldership responsibilities. We are now being seen as equals on many platforms and are valued for our insight, wisdom and discernment. However, even with all of the freedoms we enjoy, I have noticed that many born again women of God seem to still have all the hang ups and insecurities that many non-believers have as well. We are insecure, lacking confidence in who we are; in our callings and still live in realms of fear. We simply have had no understanding of the value He places on us or of our inheritance as daughters of the King. Ephesians 2:10 beautifully states "For we are His workmanship, created in Christ Jesus for good works, which God prepared beforehand that we should walk in them". It leads us to wonder what impact has a secular society had on us as born again women and our sense of self. However, even secular society is fighting back voicing displeasure in the size 0 clothing ads on very thin models. A recent soap commercial encourages women to love the body that they are in. Yet, if you asked the twenty first century women what she thought of herself based on the scripture previously stated, most, if not all would say they don't feel that way whatsoever. The majority would say in spite of the scripture, that they can find some flaw with how the look; describing themselves as not thin enough, identifying what are perceived to be physical flaws, and wishing to have what they consider attractive in other women. They can't even begin to see themselves as beautiful, never mind being made His image. This "identity crisis", if you will, is what I will explore in this women's devotional in the chapters to come. Later, in Chapter 7, we will explore a famous heroine of the Old Testament who understood and embraced all that Christ had done in her and through her.

There is joy and peace that is ours to enjoy when we can embrace all that God has for us; to completely understand the privileges we have as a child of the King. It is with this knowledge that we can become the women we are destined to be.

CHAPTER 1:

WHO ARE WE ANYWAY?

To begin with we must appreciate that God is not a respecter of persons which means His purposes, plans, mercy, grace, peace, joy and blessings are for everyone. Every man, woman and child on this planet we call home, has the incredible opportunity to embrace Him as Lord and Saviour. He doesn't discriminate and when we call on Him for blessing and favour, He is more than willing to accommodate us with extravagant love. God loves us unconditionally and as we completely yield to trusting in Him, our faith will deepen as we journey with Him. Day by day, moment by moment we will become more and more like Him as we grow in spiritual maturity. I have chosen to engage in the conversation of who we are as women in Christ and what are the promises and blessings that come with this. I have chosen passages of Scripture as reference material but one passage in particular; I would like to give considerable attention to which is from the book of Ephesians. I believe this New Testament book identifies what it is that we can have in Christ, when we come to the place where we choose Christ as our Lord and Saviour. I trust that these particular scriptures articulate what it is that we have in Christ as well as the hope and assurance that we are given as believers. We have a Father who loves and cares for His child's every need. He has incredible plans and purposes for each and every one of His children without exception. The best thing about this incredible gift is that it is free to all who ask without exception and without limits. We can call upon Him at anytime, anywhere, no matter what we have done, and receive His forgiveness and grace. It is His desire that we be fully restored, healed and made new by His love and mercy; victorious believers in every area of our lives because He freely desires us to be emotionally, physically and spiritually made whole.

Let's read Ephesians Chapter 1: 1- 14.

Paul, the author of Ephesians, beautifully addresses the saints in Ephesus with **grace and peace** "from God our Father and the Lord Jesus Christ".

"Blessed be the God, and Father of our Lord Jesus Christ who has **blessed us** with every **spiritual blessing** in the heavenly places in Christ,

just as He **chose** us in Him before the foundations of the world, that we should be holy and without blame before Him in love,

having **predestined us to adoption** as sons and daughters by Jesus Christ to Himself, according to the good pleasure of His will,

to the praise of the glory of His grace, by which He has made us **accepted** **in the Beloved**.

In Him we have **redemption** through His blood, the **forgiveness** of sins, according to the riches of His **grace** which He made to abound towards us in all wisdom and prudence,

having made known to us the mystery of His will, according to His good pleasure which He purposed in Himself.

that in the dispensation of the fullness of the times He might gather together in one all things in Christ, both which are in heaven and which are on earth in Him, in whom also we have **obtained an inheritance,** being predestined according to the purposes of Him who works all things according to the counsel of His will,

that we who first trusted in Christ should be to the praise of His glory. In Him you also trusted, after you heard the word of truth, the gospel of your salvation: in whom also, having believed, you were **sealed, with the Holy Spirit** of promise,

who is the **guarantee** of our inheritance until the redemption of the purchased possession, to the praise of His glory.

LISTENING TO GOD

Once we have decided that we are going to join forces with the King of Kings and live life in alliance with Him, according to His plans and purposes for our lives, we understand that His greatest desire is to be in constant communication with us. It is our right and privilege as a daughter of the King. He longs to be in fellowship with us and for us to know Him. God's word tells us from the very beginning that in the cool of the evening He walked and talked with Adam and Eve in the garden which He created for them to live in and rule over. Adam enjoyed an intimate relationship with the Creator of the Universe right from the beginning. Can you believe it!! God talked with Adam and Eve!

LET'S GO BACK TO THE BEGINNING

Genesis 2: 8-18, 19-23

Did you notice that Adam walked and talked with God and yet in verse 18 God stated that Adam shouldn't be alone? Thus the creation of a woman.

A woman for him to communicate with, love, create children with and live as one flesh in the Garden of Eden made just for them.

There are numerous accounts of God speaking with His children directly. Abraham, Samuel, Deborah, Daniel, Ezekiel, the apostle Paul are just a few that we can reference. Today, we can still listen and respond to the voice of the Father. John 10:27 states "My sheep listen to My voice and I know them and they follow Me." John 8:47 further validates "he who belongs to God hears what God says." This leads us to believe that we too can have intimate fellowship with the Father.

Donna Jordon in her manual "Listening to God" gives detailed instructions on how we can foster an authentic hearing and listening to God relationship.[4]

I strongly urge you, if you haven't studied her material yet, to seek out her manual and DVD series. It will truly transform how and why you communicate with Him. It is a study based on what she has walked and what she can testify to that glorifies God. In March of 2007, I attended one of her weekend seminars where I received an incredible understanding of what it means to be in relationship with God. The purpose of our

relationship with God is for listening and hearing Him which is true Christianity. The following are my notes from the seminar based on her teachings.

God working with the Holy Spirit allows us to listen to what He is saying. Working together they provide the foundation by which we can listen and hear, respond and obey to what the Father is calling us to.

HEARING GOD – A BASIC RIGHT

Hearing the voice of God is the basic right for every believer. We have every right to hear our Father's voice and to be led by the Holy Spirit who lives within us. Romans 8:14-28

"My sheep listen to My voice; and I know them and they follow Me." John 10:27

"He who belongs to God hears what God says." John 8:47

"The Lord takes the upright into His confidence." Proverbs 3:32

God communicated with men and women, who walked and talked with Him, and gave them very detailed instructions (Acts 9:10-12)

He hasn't changed. It is we who have changed. We have relied on our own thinking and man's opinions. The voice of others is so strong.

Jesus is our model. He showed us how to live and how to die.

He only did what He saw His Father doing (John 5:19-20, 30)

He only spoke as the Father told him to speak (John 8:28-29; John 12:49)

FOUR VOICES WE CAN HEAR

Our Own Voice

We must die to our own ideas, imaginations, and desires and give them to Him

"Lean not on your own understanding."
Proverbs 3:5-6

"He who trusts in himself is a fool." Proverbs 28:26;
Isaiah 5:21

When we walk close to the Lord, His desires become our desires. Psalm 37:4

Give Him our burdens. 1 Peter 5:7; Psalm 55:22;
Phil.4:6

Voice of Others

Parents, teachers, media, pastors, friends; all may have something to contribute but only look to others as much as they look to Jesus and His Word.

Voice of the Enemy

Stand against him in the all-powerful name of the Lord Jesus Christ and with the "sword of the Spirit," the Word of God.

"Submit yourselves to God, resist the devil, and he will flee from you." James 4:7

"Put on the full armor of God so that you can take your stand against the devil's schemes." Ephesians 6:11

"Resist the enemy and stand firm in the faith." 1Peter 5:6-11

Voice of God

The purpose of prayer is communication, and that leads to relationship.

We are His children (Romans 8:16)

His sheep listen to His voice (John 10:3, 4)

"I will instruct you and teach you in the way you should go; I will counsel you and watch over you." Psalm 32:8

The basis of our belief that He will speak to us comes from the knowledge of His character. He longs to communicate with us and lead us and guide us. (Isaiah 50:4-5)

God will always make a way for those who believe and obey. His truth will always set us free. (John 8:32; Psalm 84:11)

We must walk in obedience to what He has said. If we love Him, we will obey. (John 14:15, 23)

PREPARATION FOR LISTENING TO GOD

In order to hear God's voice clearly we must have surrendered, living clean and Spirit-controlled lives. It's a way of life.

Affirm Jesus's Lordship. Jesus must be Lord of your life. (Romans 10:9-10). Are you willing to do whatever He says, when He says it? We are called to do His will, not ours. (Romans 12:1,2; 2Cor 5:15)

Create in me a clean heart. Up to the knowledge you have, your heart must be right before God. (Psalm 51:10-13)

"If I had cherished sin in my heart, the Lord would not have listened." (Psalm 66:18)

Quieten yourself before God, and ask Him if there is anything hindering you from hearing from Him. He will show you by His Spirit. Tell Him how much you love Him. We need to learn to be still.

Die to your desires and ideas as to what you want to hear. Give Him your burdens and anxieties

Submit to God, resist the enemy and he has to go. (James 4:7)

Ask the Holy Spirit to come and fill you. He will reveal truth to you. (Luke 11:13; John 16:12-14)

By faith receive what He has to say to you. The righteous live by faith. Faith to believe that God does want to speak to you and faith to believe what He says. Walking with God, and fellowshipping with God, will not happen without faith.

Faith is based on the character of God and the Word of God. Faith always includes an action.

Thoughts will come into your mind, write them down. Don't argue with God or He will stop speaking, until you are finished.

Be prepared that He may speak through His Word (Psalm 119:105); or through the eyes of your heart – a vision. (Eph.1:18; Hab. 2:1)

TESTING THE WORD YOU HAVE RECEIVED

Does it go according to God's Word? (Acts17:11; 2Tim 3:16-17)

Does it glorify Jesus and bring you closer to God our Father? If prophecy exalts anyone but Jesus, be careful.

Does it witness in your spirit and with the Spirit of God? (Romans 8:6, 16)

He gives us a peace beyond our understanding (Phil 4:7; John 14:26-27)

Does it witness in the spirit of others who are in right relationship with God and who are showing the fruit of the Spirit?

God speaks...truth - He renews our thinking, that we are loved and that He wants the highest good for us. He speaks with clarity - not complicated, gently, instilling hope and establishing intimacy.

My prayer is that once you have studied the "Listening to God" material above, albeit a minimal account of the total material, that you will find value and an enlightened understanding in communication, ready to engage in and facilitate a relationship on a deeper level. This application is the foundation for your seeking, listening and journaling experiences with the Father.

DISCUSSION QUESTIONS:

What do we often think of that equates to our value and our identity in ourselves? (jobs, academics, positions in organizations)?

What does the "world" determine as someone's sense of worth?

Is this true and does this lead to peace and joy?

As women of God, can we look past the deception and see that our value is rooted in knowing we are created in His image as His daughters, knowing Jesus as our Lord and personal Savour and living in a life-giving relationship with our Creator, secure that He is deeply in love with us?

If yes, give an example?

What do you think it means to be blessed and accepted by God?

How does this matter as you live out your everyday life?

LISTENING TO GOD AND JOURNALING QUESTIONS – BASED ON EPHESIANS 1

Do you _feel_ blessed and accepted and that God loves you?

Do you _believe_ that God loves you?

Ask Jesus - what do you think and say about me?

SCRIPTURES TO MEDITATE ON

John 1: 12 received as Daughters of the King

2 Corinthians 5:17 A new creation

1 John 4:19 He first loved us

Galatians 2:20 Christ lives in me

Corinthians 5:21 Confident in who we are in Christ

Philippians 3:3 Put no confidence in the flesh

Can you come into _agreement_ with these scriptures regardless of what you believe and what you feel about yourself as an act of faith and obedience?

SOMETHING TO THINK ABOUT

"The first temptation is to question what God has said about you, the last temptation is to question who you are in Christ".

"If we can settle into these two things where we hear the voice of the Lord and we hold onto what He says regardless of circumstances, we allow the Holy Spirit to affirm out Identity as Children of God. Then all the other temptations in life lose their bite—because those who know who they are in Christ are not going to lead themselves into something self-destructing".

Bill Johnson- Bethel Church used with permission

Deborah Veuger

CHAPTER 2

GIFTS FROM THE FATHER

Let's address each of the verses and describe in detail what we can believe the scriptures are saying and how they apply to us as daughters of the King and as well, to the bride of Christ. Let's begin with the very first verse where Paul greets the Ephesus church with God's grace and peace. Paul understands that he is addressing a church that is faithful and growing in the knowledge of the Lord Jesus Christ. He is deliberate in his address to them as saints. His desire is to remind them of all the wonderful rights and privileges that they have concerning their love and their work for the Lord because they choose to remain faithful to Christ Jesus.

BLESSED WITH EVERY SPIRITUAL BLESSING

Paul goes on to remind the church that they have been blessed with every spiritual blessing in heavenly places. After considerable research by many different authors, pastors, teachers and psychologists, I've come to the conclusion that we have complete access to an inheritance purchased by Christ on the cross which includes both temporal and heavenly blessings as well. The model prayer, which we often pray, found in Matt. 6:10 states "Your will be done, on earth, as it is in Heaven" seems to validate this theme as well.

Joseph Prince elucidates "some people think that the term 'spiritual blessing' refers to only non-visible and intangible blessing like peace and joy, meaning God's promise of 'every spiritual blessing', excludes the tangible blessing of health, prosperity, a healthy marriage and so on". Joseph Prince goes on to explain "what the word 'Spiritual' means in the original Greek text, **pneumatikos**, in this context means having properties and characteristics belonging to the spirit of God".[5]

Nathan Shaw of Heart of David Ministries concurs in which he states "There has been a satanic assignment to blind the body of Christ to the spiritual blessings which are our inheritance. The church is called to be glorious but first our spiritual eyes must be open to the heavenly realms of glory. The book of Ephesians uses the term heavenly places five times, three times to refer to God's heavenly realm and twice it refers to Satan's heavenly realm. The clash between these two realms is still played out in the world and the church today."[6] If we remember that after the death of Jesus and His ascension, He went to heaven to be seated at the right hand of God and intercedes for us; therefore Jesus's death has given us full access to the infinite resources of heaven. We are so loved by our Heavenly Father that He would deny us nothing to fulfil the mandate He has given to us, His church, to display His glory. He has given each of us precious gifts from heaven to equip us to serve Him as He moves upon the earth. Eph.4:11-13 describes the types of ambassadors that He has given to the church to equip the church; the apostle, the prophet, the evangelist, the pastor and the teacher. They are called to equip the body of Christ so that we become built up until we all reach unity in the faith. They are also called for the fulfillment of the promises of God for the body of Christ and for the knowledge of the Son of God so as to become mature, attaining to the whole measure of the fullness of Christ. It is made clear that each of these five ministry positions are needed in the end return and reign of Christ. When we accept Christ as our Saviour, He has a place and position for everyone as we are all called into ministry. You might be a nurse in an NICU, an oil worker in Northern Alberta, or a provincial or federal member of parliament. Regardless of our professions or positions, all of us are called to be His witnesses and to do the work of our calling. As God has chosen us, He also anoints us, empowers us and gives us His Holy Spirit to help us fulfill all that He has planned. The work of the Holy Spirit as He dwells in us is then to comfort us, teach us and even to compensate for our weaknesses. He is our greatest source of encouragement, counsel and joy. He defends us, liberates us, convicts us and helps us spread the gospel. He brings us into worship and helps to produce the character of Christ in us.

God has equipped us for everything He wants us to do. Working by the guidance of the Holy Spirit, there is nothing that we cannot accomplish as He has placed all of the resources of Heaven at our disposal. Every spiritual blessing is ours to claim and to enjoy as He leads us to do the work for His kingdom.

CHOSEN

Paul continues by reminding them that God has chosen them, before the foundations of the world, calling them to be holy and without blame. I have read this scripture many times and one day as I was studying this passage it struck me that I didn't necessarily choose Him. Even though I remember vividly the day, as a little girl, accepting Christ as my personal Lord and Saviour and the sweetness and the blessed assurance of peace and eternal life; yet in the complex scheme of the universe He chose me!! It overwhelmed me to think that before the very foundations of the world, He knew that I would be born, where and when in history I would make my appearance. I honestly thought that I had chosen him and yet John 15:16 collaborates that "You did not choose me, but I chose you and appointed you to go and bear fruit -fruit that will last. Then the Father will give you whatever you ask in my name". Once again He makes it clear that it was He who planted us and poured out His spirit upon us so that we might be fruitful and the end result is that His Kingdom would be expanded to include new believers and ultimately that He would be glorified. It confirms that we are the children of God, His very own seed is our life line and His very own nature is within us.

PREDESTINED BY ADOPTION

Paul further encourages them with the knowledge that they were predestined by adoption as sons through Jesus Christ to Himself, according to the good pleasure of His will. We too can cling to this promise that we were predestined to live as daughters of the King. Romans 8:29 validates this as well "For whom He foreknew, He also predestined to be conformed to the image of His son, that He might be the firstborn among many brethren."

It's hard to understand that even before the world was formed God knew that His plan was for everyone to have opportunity to accept and experience the love of the Father and acceptance of His forgiveness. God wanted a family, which is made evident in the creation of Adam and Eve and His desire for them to multiply and possess the earth. God provided for them a safe, secure and a beautiful garden to call home. He also gave them significance and sense of belonging to Him. They were alive spiritually and had divine instinct as they were created in His image. They had perfect union with each other and God. God often walked in the cool of the evening with them in close fellowship. God's desire is to walk in close relationship and community with us. We all know the familiar verses of John 3:16- 17. "For God so loved the world that He gave His only begotten son, that whoever believes in Him should not perish but have ever-lasting life. For God did not send His Son into the world to condemn the world, but that the world through Him might be saved".

What sacrificial love He gave to us in exchange so that the whole world could come to experience the pure completeness of salvation.

To know that the most influential deity of all time wants to adopt us as His precious children with all the rights and privileges that come with being adopted is unfathomable.

We have nothing to give to Him, except our brokenness, sinful nature and desperate need for Him. He in turn calls us His child, His friend, and states that we are united to Him and are one in spirit with Him, He justifies us and the list goes on and on. Transformational as well, I think that's one of the most glorious promises that we are given is that we are redeemed, forgiven and complete in Him. There is nothing or no one who can complete us with perfect love other than Christ. He is perfect and He loves to validate His children. What an extraordinary God who loves us so much that He adopts us, just as we are.

Accepted in the Beloved

There is much which lies in the realm of being accepted in Christ Jesus. In Ephesians 2:13-14 we are admonished to, "Remember that you were at that time separate from Christ, excluded from the commonwealth of Israel and strangers to the covenants of promise, having no hope and without God in the world. But now in Christ Jesus you who formerly were far off have been brought near by the blood of Christ. For He himself is our peace."

The Lord tells us in I Peter 2:9-10, "But you are a chosen generation, a royal priesthood, an holy nation, a peculiar people; that you should show forth the praises of Him who hath called you out of darkness into His marvelous light; which in time past were not a people, but now are the people of God: which had not obtained mercy, but now have obtained mercy." We have been taught much about what it means to be a child of God. We have learned much about how it is by the blood of Christ that we come to God and how without His shed blood no man could call himself anything but a stranger to God as the Gentiles were once strangers to a covenant and promise which was made to Israel. Peter tells us just how accepted we are, but do we really know in our hearts what it truly means to be accepted by God? Do we really understand all that is contained in the thing we have termed "The Grace of God"?

Sigmund Freud was the first psychoanalyst who was also considered the father of understanding human behavior. Man, he said, has basic primitive wants, impulses or drives which seek expression. These, Freud called the ID, (the pleasure principle). He concluded that the strongest human desire which drives more of human life than any other, is the sex urge. This is indeed a very strong motivating force in our lives, however if we look closely we will see another desire stronger than the sex drive. It is a desire that Freud did not list. It is the desire to be accepted. The desire to be accepted is the strongest desire for most mortals and it literally dictates every area of human behavior.

The desire to be accepted by others determines what we wear, what we drive, where we go, how we act, what we do, ad infinitum.

Every religious culture that man observes yearns to be accepted by God, whatever or whomever they comprehend Him to be. Ephesians 1:6 says God accepts us completely. I do not need to live my life seeking acceptance by God, because through Jesus, He completely accepts me. We, as daughters of the King, must not miss this point in our counselling, teaching and personal revelation. Many daughters are living their lives striving to being accepted by God while many other Christians live in fear and frustration that they will not be accepted by God. We must make the choice to believe His Word which clearly states we are already accepted in Christ.

God's love and unconditional acceptance of us through the Beloved seems outside our ability to fully comprehend, yet it is ours not only to embrace but to accept and enjoy.

Within the beautiful arrangement of the song "My Beloved" by Kari Jobe, is an exquisite "ballet" set in words and tranquil music that depicts what the writer of the song eloquently captures as the Father's heart singing over His Bride. The lyrics are as follows, but if possible, listen to the song itself while reading along.

MY BELOVED

You're my beloved, you're my bride
To sing over you is my delight
Come away with me my love

Under my mercy come and wait
Till we are standing face to face
I see no stain on you my child

You're beautiful to me
So beautiful to me

I sing over you my song of peace
Cast all your cares down at my feet
Come and find your rest in me

I'll breathe my life inside of you
I'll bear you up on eagle's wings
And hide you in the shadow of my strength

I'll take you to my quiet waters
I'll restore your soul
Come rest in me and be made whole

You're my beloved, you're my bride
To sing over you is my delight
Come away with me my love [7]

Now close your eyes and imagine each and every word in this magnificent "ballet" is sung just to you! Words that capture the love our heavenly Father has for His earthly bride~ You. How marvelous, almost unfathomable can it be that He, the Master of the Universe, Creator of all living things; sun, moon, sky, rain, tides that rise and fall, and man whom He created in His own image sings over us, restores our soul and provides refuge and rest. He is beyond wonderful. In the Old Testament we can also find countless examples of God's love for His people. Isaiah writes in Isaiah 54:10 "Though the mountains be shaken and the hills be removed, yet my unfailing love for you will not be shaken nor my covenant of peace be removed, says the Lord, who has compassion on you".

The Reverend C.H. Spurgeon in a sermon title "Accepted in the Beloved" delivered on Sunday Morning, September 21, 1862 at the Metropolitan Tabernacle, Newington summarized his sermon with these words "Do not you see, Beloved, the whole way through, it is all of God and not of man? It was Christ who at first put us in His heart to be accepted there. It was the Father who put us in His Book according to the good pleasure of His own will to be accepted there. It was Christ who took us into His hands, according to His suretyship engagement, that we may be accepted there. It is

Christ who took us into His loins, begetting us again unto a lively hope that we might be accepted there. And it is Grace that has united us with the Person of Christ that we may stand accepted there".[8] Once considered a powerful sermon of the day, given one hundred and fifty two years ago, it still stands today as a complete message of truth.

Many people have told me how they could feel and experience God's love; that blankets them with a warmth which is both powerful and peaceful. I have felt the warmth of God's love also. God's love is wonderful. But sometimes we do things that sort of put us in distant places so to speak, and we can't feel the warmth of God's love shining on us. We must admit that we are the ones who put up the walls which hinder us from the warmth of God's love. Paul told the Church in Romans 8:38,39, "For I am persuaded that neither death, nor life, nor angels, nor principalities, nor powers, nor things present, nor things to come, nor height, nor depth, nor any other created thing, shall be able to separate us from the love of God, which is in Christ Jesus our Lord."

Paul's strong statement determines that we can do nothing that will separate us from the Fathers perfect love and plan for us. If we die in Christ, we are lifted up into our eternal home never to be physically separated from Him again. If we are in

Christ, there is nothing past, present, or future that can expel us from His divine gift of acceptance into His family and His presence. Once we are found in covenant relationship with the Father, and our hearts desire and motive is to love and serve Him with all of our heart, soul and mind, we are guaranteed that we will always have a relationship and place in the family of God as well as the eternal promise of going home to Heaven to be with Jesus and other believers who have gone ahead of us.

2 Corinthians 5:17 beautifully declares that "if any man is in Christ, he is a new creation; old things passed away; behold, all thing have become new." What a reassuring promise of God. Note that it states that once we are in Christ we are a new creation, accepted and loved in every way. Jesus is the only one in the world that can make that statement and follow through with it. His promise of new life cannot only be felt physically on dedication of ourselves to Christ, but it is experienced supernaturally when the desires of the world no longer entice and ensnare us. The scales literally fall off our eyes to see with true vision of the life that Christ has set out for us. Oswald Chambers' classic "My UTMOST for His HIGHEST" devotional (1935, April 2) illustrates the life of Paul's conversion from Saul also known as Paul in Acts 9:17. Oswald states that

"when Paul received his sight, he received spiritually an insight into the Person of Jesus Christ and the whole of his subsequent life and preaching was nothing but Jesus Christ."[9] The verse itself bears witness that upon Paul's conversion, immediately there fell from his eyes something like scales and he received his sight at once; and he arose and was baptised. The promise of newness is like a cup of cold water to a thirsty man. Christ takes our sinful nature and transforms us into His image. Our transformation is nothing short of miraculous as we exchange the old man for the new man; a divine intervention as decided and as glorious as when God created all things out of nothing.

DISCUSSION QUESTION:

Re-read the first few verses of scripture of Ephesians 1:1-6.

What stands out to you in verse 3 that is ours to receive freely from the Father as a gift from Him? What does He call us?

What makes you feel insecure and compelled to compare yourself to others around you?

Can you recall a time when you felt belittled, threatened or even jealous around someone else you perceived to be better than you?

After listening to My Beloved, or simply by reading the lyrics, do you have a greater revelation of God's love for you?

1 John 4:18 says "There is no fear in love; but perfect love casts out fear". So if we believe this why do we still feel badly about ourselves?

LISTENING TO GOD AND JOURNALING QUESTIONS

Philippians 3:3 say that as believers we "worship God in Spirit and by the Spirit of God, and exult and glory and pride ourselves in Jesus Christ and put no confidence or dependence (on what we are) in the flesh and on outward privileges and physical advantages and external appearances." (AMP)

Ask God who He sees you placing your confidence in and if there needs to be some changes, to show you where and to help you with them.

Ask Jesus how He accepts you and calls you blessed?

Jesus sees you as a unique creation, and I want to encourage you to value and respect the person He made you to be. I'm not talking about accepting sin in your life but rather accept who He made you to be in Him.

Ask Him what He values about you?

SCRIPTURES TO MEDITATE ON

1 Peter 1:23 I am God's child

Romans 6:11 I am a Spirit being

1 Peter 2:9 I am chosen

1 Thessalonians 1:4 I am greatly loved by God

SOMETHING TO THINK ABOUT:

"Chosen by God, bearing the fruit of the Spirit, abiding in Christ"; all of these mark our identity as new creatures in the Lord. God did not save us simply to improve our behavior, but to bring us into complete transformation. In Christ we have been totally remade, brand-new from the inside out."

Mary Audrey Raycroft used with permission

CHAPTER 3

REDEMPTION, FORGIVENESS AND GRACE

"But God demonstrated His own love for us that while we were yet sinners Christ died for us". Romans 5:8

Jesus extends to us His full redemption through His precious blood, shed on Calvary so that we can be called the Children of God. Paul carried on to state further that we are forgiven of our sins; past, present and future, because God so desired to extend His rich grace towards us.

In the Easter season it becomes poignantly clear that this unselfish act of love spared you and me from an eternity without Christ. We know that the Cross offers complete and total redemption as we contemplate the celebration of His death and ultimate resurrection on the third day. We also reflect on the consequences of our sin and what His sacrifice accomplished. It released us from the chains of slavery which we indisputably deserved, into a new found redemption and forgiveness of sin. This unites us with Him in His death and enables us to walk in the newness of life through our Saviour and Lord Jesus Christ.

Romans 6:23 "For the wages of sin is death, but the gift of God is eternal life through our Lord and Saviour Jesus Christ".

God's forgiveness of sin and His gift of grace is nothing short of miraculous. Forgiveness by a Holy God, who does so without exception and without condition is true to His character and nature. He forgives the sins of an innocent child the same as a mass murderer like Jeffery Dahmer, whose acts of cannibalism and sadistic murder of eleven innocent victims made headlines in 1991. Dahmer later professed a relationship with Christ and was baptised in a prison whirlpool a few months before he was killed in November, 1994 by another inmate. Nothing is unpardonable to Him. It seems incomprehensible that God could so willingly extend complete and total forgiveness to such a cruel man and yet, if we are honest we don't need to look very hard to discover our own sinful nature and need for Christ for as they say, murder begins in the heart.

Forgiveness can be one of the hardest personal freedoms that is ours to give away because of our old nature as well as the voice of the enemy that strategically wants to deceive us, keeping us in the bondage of unforgiveness. We must endeavor to operate like free women, by affirming that we are no longer controlled by our old master. We have been set free from sins' slavery and we need to see ourselves as free. We can receive the forgiveness of sins and the grace He gives. Our positions are sheltered in Christ, no room for fear and nothing to be ashamed of. Once we choose to renew our minds from an old way of thinking to the newness we have in Christ, we will be set free from the feelings of shame, failure, sin and disgrace into His forgiveness, His grace, His mercy and His love. I don't know about you, but in my life I have unintentionally and selfishly, intentionally, hurt people. I have lived with the shame and the consequences of those choices. I found it easier to forgive others that have hurt me rather than to forgive myself when I've intentionally or unintentionally hurt others. My prayer as I mature in Him, is that I want to be more like Jesus when dealing with others and forgiving of myself as He is with me.

In Philips Yancey's book 'What's So Amazing About Grace' He states "Grace means there is nothing we can do to make God love us more - no amount of spiritual calisthenics, and renunciations, no amount of knowledge gained from seminaries and divinity schools, no amount of crusading on behalf of righteous causes. And grace means there is nothing we can do to make God love us less—no amount of racism or pride, pornography or adultery or even murder. Grace means that God already loves us as much as an infinite God can possibly love". "Grace teaches us that God loves because of who God is, not because of who we are". "Categories of worthiness do not apply."[10]

An Inheritance

A few years ago a relative of mine left me an inheritance of significant monies which was to be considered as gifted, not according to the laws of the land as taxable funds. In other words, after a year of waiting for Probate, which is the first step in the legal process of administering the estate of a deceased person, resolving all claims and distributing the deceased person's property under a will, we received an inheritance. A probate court decides the legal legitimacy of a testator's will and grants its approval by granting probate to the executor. The probated will becomes a legal instrument that may be enforced by the executor in the law courts if necessary. A probate also officially appoints the executor (or personal representative), generally named in the will, as having legal power to dispose of the testator's assets in the manner detailed in the testator's will. Once we were informed by the lawyer of the deceased, and also by the executor of the will, that matters had been finally settled in the Estate, we were given an amount of money according to the wishes of my deceased relative. In other words, we received an inheritance that we did not earn nor had expected. It was a gift that would not ever be repaid.

God too gives us an inheritance that He has prearranged for us to enjoy as children of the King. It is an unconditional, with no expectations, everyone included gift. Royalty as well as the extremely impoverished man on the street with nothing but a cart full of soda cans; without exemption, all are invited and are equal shareholders of this magnificent life to come. No one is denied regardless of position. A seasoned believer or a last minute conversion, like the thief on the cross, who in the final hours recognised Jesus as the Christ and asked to be remembered.

Both have every right legally to be added into the family of Christ and ultimately into Heaven. It is a tremendous gift, totally undeserved but gratefully accepted.

Our directive is only that we must realize the fullness of this inheritance, which makes us brothers with Christ, members of His household and therefore; heirs and recipients with him of all Our Father's riches. Gal.4:7. It causes our Heavenly Father great joy when we choose to appropriate our inheritance and it shows the world that His son's death was not in vain. It shows the world how great His love, mercy and how generous He truly is to His children.

Can you imagine if I had chosen instead to take the inheritance that I had been given and decided that I would not enjoy it, even so much as to just leave it in the bank and never think of it again. That's not what it was intended for. It was meant to be utilized and enjoyed by me.

God's inheritance is also understood to be accepted, enjoyed and given to us here as well as for Eternity. It is the reward of a satiating relationship with Him, not just now but for Eternity.

Sealed, with the Holy Spirit of promise; guaranteed

Historical digs have proven that even in the earliest centuries, including the times of Ancient Egypt, the people incorporated seals in the form of signet rings. Some with the names of kings have even been found. Because they were used to attest to the authority of its bearer, the ring was also seen as a symbol of a king's power, which is one explanation for its inclusion in the regalia of certain monarchies. When a king sent out a written message, the message was sealed with wax and the monarch's signet ring was then stamped into the wax. It was sealed to display his authority as king and it was a sign of authenticity. The wax assured that the sealed document would only be opened by the recipient of the document and it would give assurance that it hadn't been tampered with.

The Christian believer today also has an eternal guarantee from our Lord Jesus as we are valued by Him. He has given us the assurance of the Holy Spirit by placing Him in us as a seal and as a further guarantee that His promises are true and are from everlasting to everlasting.

It is also indicative of ownership as you don't place your seal on something that isn't yours. We are distinguished from others by His seal as He has set us apart to Himself, with His purposes in mind.

A seal also designates something of value. God doesn't just seal anything that is not of importance to Him but only that which He puts a high value on. He treasures us. Every year I make jam and in the process of making this delicious spread, the jam must set up and the jars must seal to preserve the jam which keeps it from mold and bacteria that would grow if not properly sealed. When we are born again, God seals us by His Holy Spirit and nothing can break that seal.

John Piper states this "If the Spirit seals shut, the point must be that He seals in faith and seals out unbelief and apostasy. If the Spirit seals us as a sign of authenticity, then He is that sign and it is the Spirit's work in our life which is God's trademark. Our eternal sonship is real and authentic if we have the Spirit. He is the sign of divine reality in our lives".[11]

2 Tim. 2:19 assures us that "Nevertheless the solid foundation of God stands, having this seal: '"The Lord knows those who are His" and "Let everyone who names the name of Christ depart from iniquity"'.

As we conclude the passages of scripture from Ephesians, there can be no doubt of the Father's unceasing, never wavering, consistent and constant love that He has for His Bride. The promises in Him are extravagant and well beyond what we deserve, and I know that I'm incredibly grateful to possess and enjoy them. The pleasure of just doing everyday life with Him supersedes all expectations of what this world could even begin to offer. God has promised us His grace, by which He also adds mercy; with the ultimate reward of Eternity. This should make even the hardest of hearts warm.

DISCUSSION QUESTIONS:

Does the passage of Ephesians 1 resonate in your spirit as truth?

Not just for everyone else.... but for you personally?

Which "gift" stands out the most to you that our heavenly Father has given us?

Why?

Do you believe that you are "sealed" with an eternal seal? What do you think that this is?

What do you think about your inheritance?

(Colossians 1:12 tells us that the Father has qualified us to be partakers of the inheritance).

What do you think about your Eternity?

(Colossians 1:22- stated that He presents us holy and blameless and irreproachable in His sight)

Do you believe that you are forgiven of all your sins, past, present and even future?

LISTENING TO GOD AND JOURNALING QUESTIONS

We know that the father of all lies is the enemy or Satan. What lies about yourself have you believed to be true, based on your belief systems about yourself?

What does Jesus say to you about them?

You now know and can see that this faulty belief system limits you from receiving all that the Father has for you. What steps will you take to ask the Father to renew your mind, take every thought captive so that you can walk in all that He wants to give you? Ask Jesus to help you.

SCRIPTURES TO MEDITATE ON:

Colossians 3:9-10 Put off the old man/woman

Romans 1:7; Ephesians 2:4; Colossians 3:12; 1 Thessalonians 1:4 I am greatly loved by God

2 Corinthians 5:17 I am a new creation

2 Corinthians 5:21 I am the righteousness of God

Romans 5:17 Received the gift of Righteousness

Philippians 4:19 I lack for nothing

Romans 12:2 Renewed mind

SOMETHING TO THINK ABOUT:

The understanding of grace, forgiveness, mercy, the unconditional love of God and the doctrine of righteousness through Christ is the foundation for everything else in our relationship with and service to God. We must be rooted deeply in the unconditional love of God, know with certainty that His attitude toward us is merciful and have revelation of who we are "in Christ".

Joyce Meyers used with Permission

CHAPTER 4

YET WE STRUGGLE

Yet many of us struggle with the full acceptance of the Fathers love and His great mercies that He extends to us. Romans 5:1 reassures us that once we come to the conclusion that we have been justified by faith, we have peace with God through Jesus Christ. If we stop and meditate on this promise, we just might realize that faith is a foundational stone that helps us to build the dwelling place that Christ can reside in us.

What keeps us at arm's length from experiencing the fullness of God? If we are honest we know that it is sin that hinders our fellowship with God. Whether it be some gross moral sin like murder or a sin of the mind, pride, envy or jealousy; sin seems to be that one thing that puts up the walls which make us incapable of feeling the warmth and acceptance of God's love. Before we accepted Christ, we were enemies of Him, however, once we came into relationship with Him through the blood of His son; we were reconciled with the Father. We no longer need to have fear of an angry, stoic and detached God but rather we come into the presence of a merciful, concerned and engaging Father who sent His only son to pay the penalty of sin and death, through Him on the Cross. The cross assures our salvation and redemption. The cross reassures us of His peace, His protection and His unrelenting forgiveness of sin. We can come to Him not fearing His anger but rather experiencing His loving correction and assurance of forgiveness of our sin. Lam.3:22-24 confirms this with another promise, "Through the Lord's mercies we are not consumed, because His compassions fail not. They are new every morning; great is your faithfulness. The Lord is my portion, says my soul, therefore I hope in Him".

We now have the authority to come boldly before the throne room of Christ as a child of the King. He is our Daddy. He is our redemption. He gives us peace.

Why then do we feel unloved by God? Is it because we don't spend the time necessary in fellowship with Jesus, whether it is in His word or perhaps in our prayer time, maybe even both? So many Christians, when they sin, feel driven away from God when we should be able to run towards His great love, with a repentant heart. I have known believers who have allowed the lies of the enemy to keep them from fully experiencing His love, His grace and forgiveness and have walked away from His church and even eventually from their Lord and Saviour.

But, one has to wonder what are other issues, experiences and situations that keep Christ followers from enjoying all that we have in Christ. Others whose experiences in life, in the church and in their Christian walk with the Lord, have left them in pain, sceptical, even cynical, with feelings of rejection and negative in conjecture, feeling helpless and hopeless in most situations in life. In Jesus' day they were called Pharisees, we label them as cynics.

This is not to say that those who have experienced emotional or physical abuse are of the above category but rather are considered victims of those left in charge of their well-being. Children of abuse are often a product of a very dysfunctional childhood. Their pain has often carried them into adulthood as cynical, if not for the intervention of Jesus as He deals with the emotional pains of their abusive past. We will discuss this further in the next chapter.

Charles Swindoll, in his book "The Grace Awakening" describes this persona in such detailed liberty as "killers on the loose today". "The problem is that you can't tell by looking. They don't wear little buttons that give away their identity, nor do they carry signs warning everybody to stay away. On the contrary, a lot of them carry Bibles and appear to be clean-living, nice-looking, law-abiding citizens. Most of them spend a lot of time in churches, some in places of religious leadership. Many are so respected in the community; their neighbors would never guess they are living next door to killers. They kill freedom, spontaneity, and creativity; they kill joy as well as productivity. They kill with their words and their pens and their looks. They kill with their attitudes far more often than with their behavior. There is hardly a church or Christian organization or Christian school or missionary group or media ministry where such danger does not lurk."[12]

Often it's our faulty view of God; that we see Him as incapable of taking care of our needs or that He will open a wonderful door of opportunity only to slam it shut once we enter through the threshold causing us further pain and humiliation. The truth lies in a faulty belief system, our own fears and perceptions of who He is, not who He really is a loving, concerned God. We choose to walk by faith, to see that He is the creator of every opportunity and master of every mission. He loves to open doors that we need only walk through. He wants to go with us guiding us and cheering us on to new heights of achievement and revelation as to who He is in every situation. He invests in us to build character and faith in our own God-given abilities and talents that He has given us. He wants to build trust and waits for us to take the small steps of faith in the direction of His calling and leading. It occurred to me that the American coin has stamped on it "In God we Trust" and yet one often wonders if this truth is stamped on the believer's heart. The irony of this all is that God is the one who is truly trustworthy and it is we, His people, that are the least trustworthy. Yet, He is more than willing to take a chance on us, willing to wait until we decide to engage Him in all of life's matters and struggles. Often, it is in what we perceive as insurmountable obstacles that God turns them into exciting and promising opportunities which have been disguised as problems. We often think that resistance, opposition, trials and tribulations; adversity on every side is then not the plan of God. We are disillusioned into thinking that we have not heard from God but it is rather the opposite, if indeed this is an open door we are to go through. Yet the Apostle Paul anticipated challenges when he recorded in 1 Cor. 16:18-19 "I will tarry in Ephesus until Pentecost. For a great and effective door has opened to me, and there are many adversaries". According to Paul's letters, a sign of adversity is often an indication that indeed you are in the right place where God wants you. No worthwhile attempt will go unchallenged. Opportunity and opposition are natural counterparts.

Fear is another culprit that raises the hairs on the back of your neck wanting to leave you paralyzed to move forward in any clear direction but panic. It is sufficient to say that if we do not take the hand of the Father as He leads us into opportunities, regardless of the nervous, scared emotions that tend to rise to the surface when the path is uncertain, we will fail to miss the exhilarating thrill of the victorious outcome of His plans and purpose. We must determine to trust His promises and take the steps of faith that will lead us into closer relationship with Him. We must remember not to take our eyes off of Him during the journey.

Writing this book was scary for me! I knew that Jesus had lead me through every part of the process, yet writing it was such an unknown. My fear was, was I communicating His heart? Would it be engaging and most importantly would the reader read this book, and listen to hear His voice speak just to them, would they feel His heart and awesome love for them? When it was almost finished my father passed away, and with a very sad heart, I laid it down to grieve. So you see, we all experience fears, doubts and challenges.

However, just as there can and often will be great adversity experienced in walking through the doors of opportunity that God has called us to, there is much blessing and great dividends in time and for eternity. Think of the many missionary women that crossed the ocean to spread the Gospel to an unknown population. One of these was Dr. Clara Swain, the first woman medical missionary appointed to a field in India in 1870. "Beaver makes it clear that Swain and others saw no separation between their medical and evangelist work. Their manifestation of loving concern for their patients as individuals, and their meditation of the love of God in Christ for persons were as important as their scientific

knowledge and technical skill. The writings and speeches of the women medical missionaries make it clear that they considered themselves evangelists."[13]

"Many of these pioneering missionary women made significant results in the status women, which in many cultures was very low and had almost no rights. Missionary women, usually single, evangelized them, teaching them to see themselves as children of God. These women and girls were then encouraged to study, develop their gifts and in some cases, enter professions such as education and medicine". [14]

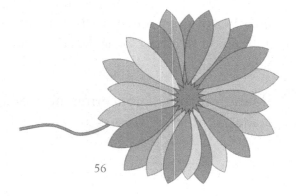

DISCUSSION QUESTIONS:

Do you think as a Christian society that we have created a "self-sufficient" attitude relying on ourselves instead of Christ to change us?

Are we striving to change ourselves instead of relying on the power of the Holy Spirit to transform us into the image of Christ?

Do you sometimes find yourself cynical and critical? What triggers this negative response?

If we rely on Christ to transform us, is it then necessary to understand who He created us to be in order to fulfill the mandate the He has personally designed for each of us?

Do you have past trauma from childhood or previous experiences that hinders you? Rejection, abuse, dysfunction, emotional pain?

Can you forgive as Christ has forgiven you? (Based on Matthew 6:14)

Can you see your past in the light of who you are in Christ, understanding that you are no longer a product of your past? You are a product of Christ's work in the cross – a new creation. You have the privilege of evaluating your past experiences in the light of who you are today!

LISTENING TO GOD AND JOURNALING QUESTIONS:

Ask Jesus to bring to remembrance any past or childhood pain that He wants to deal with and listen for His response. When you ask Jesus to search your heart, He will bring into remembrance those dark areas of your past and bring them to light, into His healing and at the right time.

Do you still struggle with thoughts of inadequacy and insecurity?

What other faulty belief and perceptions do you struggle with that do not line up with God's word and yet sometimes you still believe them?

What do you fear?

Do you fully engage in the grace that we are given as daughters of the King?

Knowing what you know today, with what we have covered so far and your journaling and listening to God, is there anything still that hinders you?

SCRIPTURES TO MEDITATE ON:

Ephesians 1:17-18 I have received the spirit of wisdom and revelation of Jesus

Colossians 2:10 I am complete in Him

Romans 8:17 We are more than conquerors

Romans 8: 31-39 What can separate us from the Love of Christ?

Revelation 12:11 I am an overcomer by the blood of the Lamb.

2 Timothy 1:7 God has not given us a spirit of fear...

Isaiah 55: 12 I will go out in joy and be led forth in peace

SOMETHING TO THINK ABOUT:

"Too many Christians identify with the first Adam –with the Adam who sinned and was exiled from the presence of God. In reality, however, Christians are to be identified with Jesus Christ, the last Adam. As a result the difference between the two Adams in your history in eternally profound. You need to be sure you're identifying with the right Adam, with Jesus your Savior." [15]

Dr. Neil Anderson used with Permission

Deborah Veuger

CHAPTER 5

A TRUSTWORTHY FATHER

Many counsellors in practises around the world are treating women whose identities and sense of self-worth have been confused or crushed due to an emotionally or verbally abusive, or absentee father or male role model in their lives. They quietly, sometimes tearfully express the profound and lasting impact that has often carried them into adulthood and into their marriages. Their misconceived ideas of what their Heavenly Father looks like are based on how their earthly fathers treated them. Their fathers may have shown uncontrollable angry outbursts and people scattered in fear at the first signs of their emotional tirades and the unrealistic expectations to always keep daddy happy was more than a child, adolescent and young women was meant to bear. It resembled a faulty and flawed picture of any woman's Heavenly Father's character. Her belief and fear is that not only is God angry with her, there is nothing that she can do to ever please Him. She has a complete misunderstanding that there are times that God does get angry, but He is not an angry God, quite the contrary. She may feel the need to suppress all anger, justified or not for fear of becoming like her father so she lives with unrealistic emotional responses to many of life's struggles and challenges.

Her father might have been distant and aloof to all of her affections and even deliberately withholding love leaving her longing for love from him. She can't help the feelings of rejection and emotional pain. Wanting to please him, going to great lengths to try to earn his love, but subconsciously knowing that she doesn't quite measure up.

Her earthly father may have physically and/or sexually abused her leaving her so emotionally scared that every part of her sexual identity is now warped, opening up feelings and confusing desires long before they were intended to be. Feelings of shame and guilt and the need to keep everything a secret, scarred before she even has the joy of experiencing the pure delight of intimacy intended only for the marriage bed.

It should be noted that "95% of child sexual abuse perpetrated on children are by someone they know further eroding the matters of trust with someone they felt safe and secure with.

"Inappropriate boundary crossings" are by someone they know and trust, the symptoms are layered with the complexity of the repercussions of betrayal. Even if not admonished or (threatened) to keep the assault secret, children often do not tell due to embarrassment, shame and guilt. In their naiveté they mistakenly assume that they are "bad". They carry the shame that belongs to the molester. In addition, children fear punishment and reprisal. They frequently anguish over "betraying" someone who is part of their family or social circle and fantasize what might happen to their perpetrator. This is especially true if it is a family member they are dependent on".[16]

How imperative it is to teach our children that they have rights and freedoms and that no one regardless of who they are, has the right to make them feel uncomfortable regarding their bodies. They should be taught that they need to trust and act on their own instincts reducing the risks to sexual violation.

Sexual Trauma is a sacred wound - an intrusion into our inmost being and violation of our God inspired private parts. We must defend and honor their rights to personal space, and privacy. Letting them know that they have the right to be in charge of their little bodies through protecting them from the unwanted attention of cheek pinching, lap sitting and unwanted kisses to please the adults in their lives.

Joyce Meyers, in her book "God is Not Mad at You" recalls from her own horrific childhood and in her own words states "I am sure that at the beginning of my father's sexual abuse towards me I was ashamed of what he was doing, and I clearly remember feeling guilty, even though I was too small to understand why I felt that way. At some point, as the abuse continued, I took the shame inside myself, and I became ashamed of me because he was abusing me...Over the many years of abuse, I had developed a shame based nature." Shame is actually much deeper and more damaging than guilt. I was not able to heal from the abuse in my childhood until I realized that I had toxic shame filling my soul. I was ashamed of who I was and it poisoned everything in my life".[16]

Psalm 34:17-18 comforts us with the promise "The righteous cry out, and the Lord hears them and delivers them out of all their troubles. The Lord is near to those who have a broken heart. And saves such as have a contrite spirit".

It is safe to say that God wants to comfort us and reassure us that He has not only heard our cries but His desire is to rescue and restore us. He understands our pain and contrite spirit and longs to make right the wrongs that have happened against us. He is the perfect Father and will never mistreat or abuse His child. If we can take the step of faith and reach out to trust, He will undoubtedly heal and restore all the pain and dysfunction of the past. Once we choose the promises of the Father, to trust that He and His words are true, we will journey through a process of healing and restoration. Isaiah 61:1, 7 reassures us "He has sent Me to heal the broken hearted, to proclaim liberty to the captives and the opening of the prison to those who are bound. Instead of your shame you shall have double honor, and instead of confusion they shall rejoice in their portion. Everlasting joy shall be theirs".

Is this perhaps a journey towards healing? Clearly there will be lifelong implications. However, the beauty of our Lord and Saviour is that He will lead us into paths of wholeness and emotional wellness.

Every part of Him wants to forgive, to redeem and restore. Isaiah 51:11 "Therefore the redeemed of the Lord shall return, and come with singing unto Zion, and everlasting joy shall be upon their heads. They shall obtain gladness and joy, and sorrow and mourning shall flee away".

Isaiah proclaims the hope that God does redeem, and with that comes singing and an everlasting joy that is guaranteed. God's love for us is so passionate that He takes the trials and the tribulations of this world which have left us feeling defeated and overwhelmed and replaces them with gladness. He takes our feelings of distrust; our past failures and inevitable discouragement and in turn replacing them with joy; dispelling our sadness and causing our mourning to flee away. Not <u>maybe</u> will flee away, but <u>will</u> flee away! God promises us to heal the mistrust, with healing balms of joy. Renewing the mind with thoughts of hope, filling us with trust and establishing a firm foundation based on **His** trustworthiness. So, once we have established that He wants us to trust Him completely in our relationship with Him, we can step out into new found belief systems that give us peace and joy as a daughter of the King. We can believe that His word and the scriptures are true, reliable and inherently filled with promises that He keeps. He will heal the damaged emotions as you journey with Him on the pathway of total healing.

I know that these promises are true, because I too endured child sexual abuse from a relative, thankfully not my father who was a wonderful man of God, not perfect but completely forgiven as my dad now walks with my mom and Jesus in Heaven. Rather a relative given access to me who then proceeded to molest me from a very young age to raping me when I was eight years old, left in a field, to be discovered by my grandfather. I must be honest to say that this has had an effect on me my whole life, but with Jesus and His healing over many years, this tragic event does not define me.

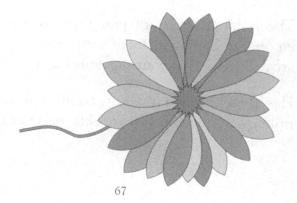

DISCUSSION QUESTIONS:

Please note that this is not to make you feel uncomfortable as you need only share what you are emotionally able to. Only disclose what you feel safe to share.

Do you struggle with the picture of what or who God is? Is He angry towards you?

Unloving?

How do you think God intends for you to resolve those past traumas?

Some emotional wounds and traumas can leave you holding a lot of emotional baggage. Consider how emotions from the past may be affecting you today?

What names evoke a positive emotional reaction from you?

What names bring up negative emotions from you?

The residual effects of past traumas are primary emotions. The intensity of your primary emotions are determined by your previous life history.

Has there been a present event that triggers a primary emotion? If you are able, be specific.

Do you find that sometimes how you react to certain situations now, is a conscious or unconscious reaction from a past wound?

Remember that there is a relationship between emotions and beliefs. Keep in mind that the intensity of the primary emotion is determined by how you perceive the event at the time it happens. Explain how this truth can help you deal with the primary emotions rooted in your past?

God knows about the hidden hurts within you that you may not be able to see. You can trust Him to be by your side as you feel the emotions

from the past and also trust Him to free you from their effects on your life. Know that the Holy Spirit will guide you into all truth. John 16:13.

LISTENING TO GOD AND JOURNALING QUESTIONS

If the hurts happened before you were a believer, you can find hope in the fact that as a Christian, you are a new creation in Christ. Old things including the traumas and the emotions of the traumas are passes away. Spend some time talking to God, journaling and listening, asking Him to help you to believe in that newness as you deal with the emotions and hurts from your past.

Ask Jesus to help you in perceiving painful events of the past from the perspective of your new identity in Christ; seeing it as the beginning process of healing damaged emotions.

Realizing that forgiveness is a necessary step to healing and wholeness, can you ask the Father to help you forgive the offender(s) so that the enemy cannot get a foot hold or place a wedge in your heart. God will help you and heal you.

SCRIPTURES TO MEDITATE ON:

Psalm 139:23 Search me O God

Isaiah 53:5 1 Peter 2:24 I am healed

Colossians 1:11 I am strengthened

James 4:7 I am submitted to God and the devil flees

Deuteronomy 28:13 I am the head and not the tail

Isaiah 54:14 - I am far from oppression and fear

SOMETHING TO THINK ABOUT:

There is a beautiful exchange in heavenly places when we allow the Wonderful Counsellor to quietly come in and wipe away all of our tears, comfort us in our anxieties and fears and replace them with His everlasting peace, and immeasurable joy. It is then we experience the fullness of the Cross and His resurrection, knowing He fully understands our pains of this brief life. The enemy is defeated and we walk in wholeness and healing.... with beautiful scars.

Debra Veuger

Deborah Veuger

CHAPTER 6

INTENTIONAL LIVING

It is wonderful to know that we are unconditionally loved and accepted by God. It frees us up to believe that God's plans and purposes are for us; YES!!

It helps us to know that with our faith placed firmly and with confidence in Him, He does want us to live intentional and fruitful lives. Trusting that from the very beginning when He created Adam and Eve, it was with the instructions to go and live a purposeful and joy-filled life. I believe that God wants us to understand who He created us to be for this very purpose.

Even before we were "formed in our mothers' wombs - He knew us". The date and time we would be born; where we would live, our eye colour, hair colour and whether we would be tall or short. Even further He took the time to develop in us our strengths, our personality types and even the friendships we would have and the endless possibility for careers that we could have in order to "bring home the bacon" and bring Him honor. There is not one detail, not one surprise that was not already part of His plan!

Jesus is the source of our strengths and we know that as we are "fearfully and wonderfully made". Psalm 139:14. We also know that He is going to allow life's sufferings and struggles to develop our strengths even more. The best part is that He walks with us and helps us. He also has created us with certain weaknesses so that "His power is made perfect in our weakness" 2 Corinthians 12:9. In other words, we need Him to help us fulfill and to divinely show us how to operate and walk with the talents, gifts, strengths and unique personality He has given to each of us.

With that wonderful knowledge let's explore who we are in terms of personality types and strengths.

One website where you can do a personality profile which is a 92 DISC and Spiritual Gifts Profile is: _https://www.**arcchurches**.com/**disc**_

You can also explore in depth many DVD series, such as the DISC personality system and discover what type you are. It's so exciting to truly understand yourself and others.

For Strengthfinders, You can purchase this valuable tool at Chapters, Amazon, Barnes and Noble. Inside the book your will find a unique access code which will give you a questionnaire that you fill out that in turn identifies your 5 top strengths. This is a wonderful tool that will help you to focus and develop your natural God-given strengths instead of always being discouraged by trying to work on your weaknesses. This is truly powerful and positive.

If you are doing this book with a Life group, once you have taken both of these questionnaires, please bring them to the next week's sessions and you can talk about each of your individual strengths.

If you plan to do this by yourself, tell a friend what you discovered about yourself and celebrate the uniqueness of you.

DISCUSSION QUESTIONS:

Are you surprised about anything that was revealed regarding your DISC personality?

Spiritual Gifts? Does it make you think twice about where you would volunteer or serve, or even pursue as a career based on the information that you received?

What was one strength that surprised you?

Delighted you?

Felt incredible relief with?

Can you see where practical skills are also designed to get the work done lead by the Holy Spirit?

Do you see how you are uniquely created to serve in the Body of Christ as in unison not in competition?

Can you see that when we have an understanding of who and what we are called to be, there is no room for jealousy in the body?

Do you see how God designed each of us differently to serve and meet the needs of His people and His church?

LISTENING TO GOD

Knowing now that you have a better understanding of your strengths, gifts and personality, ask Jesus what to do with them?

Freedom comes from knowing that we do not need to live in the power of striving to live in our strengths, but rather from Jesus as our source of strength. Ask Jesus how He would like you to use your strengths to glorify Him and serve others? And if you mess up (and you will) ask His forgiveness and keep on going.

Ask Him to help you not to slip into the patterns of comparisons, but rather to keep your focus on how your gifts are just for you, created by Him.

SCRIPTURES TO MEDITATE ON:

Luke 14:28-30 Administration

Romans 12:7 Service

Acts 5:1-11 Gift of Knowledge or discernment

Acts 2:37-40 Gift of Prophecy

John 10: 1-8 Shepherding

SOMETHING TO THINK ABOUT:

"Yes, our skills, personalities and strengths matter. Yes, they are important to God's purpose for our lives. But in the end, what He wants most is simply us. Our hearts, our dreams, our days and nights. Then what we do with our skills is just a natural response - and ordinary activities such as cooking or cleaning become just as sacred as leading a church or going on a mission trip."

Holley Gerth Used with Permission

CHAPTER 7

ESTHER- WOMAN OF INFLUENCE

Over the last couple of chapters we have explored what the word of God says about who Jesus is and what He has done for us. We have also discovered who we are in Christ and from now on in, who we see ourselves in the revelations of who we are in Christ. It is from this paradigm or frame of reference that we as well look into the word of God to discover once again heroines that learned like we did, about their identity in Jesus and His destiny for them. There are many well-known women that I could have considered for this chapter that have greatly influenced both past and present world events. These women have had an opportunity to speak into the lives of people who had the power to make changes on the world stage, or they are women who have risen up to their callings that have been placed on them to impact all those who come into their realm of influence. The woman that I chose was Esther.

Esther was a woman, found in the Old Testament who risked great danger, personal hardship and paid a price for the destiny that she chose to fulfill. It cost her and yet she chose to be the woman that was needed to change the destiny of her life and that of her Jewish people. Esther was not only courageous but determined even if it meant great personal risk and sacrifice to save her nation and the future nations of God's people.

If we thought that the first "Bachelor" episode was created by ABC reality television back in 2002, one would have to point to the story of Esther to correct that assumption. It seems that back in the Persian dynasty, they had their own version of "reality dating and marriage" drama, except theirs, meaning the bride to be, came with a year's preparation and no one backed out or said no to the king, that is, if they didn't want to be banished forever.

This true story takes place back in the years thought between 486-465 BC, in the winter palace of King Ahasuerus also known as Emperor Xeres, in the city of Susa. "Two lavish banquets were being held. "One banquet, by the present Queen Vashti, which included the women of the court and nobility; the other by her husband, the King, for his councillors and all the men of Susa." [17] It seems that the king's banquet was in full swing with much wine and with that came much merriment. Under that influence and with the urging of his drunken courts men, the king sent for his queen to appear before the men at his banquet. It needs to be noted that most women present at the king's banquet would be prostitutes and there would be many of them. Women invited would not be there to enjoy the banquet, but rather, to be used by the men present. We really do not know the King's intentions other than Vashti was described as very beautiful and it was thought that the king might have wanted to show her off to the men of the city. The Queen of the Persian Empire was thought to have been chosen from among seven ancient and noble lineages. It would have been considered beneath her and embarrassing for her to be paraded before a very large crowd of drunken men. It was not a suitable thing for a Queen to do and if her husband had had his senses about him he would not have requested that of her. She knew all too well that when husbands and wives did dine together, with much wine flowing, the wives were requested to leave as they were replaced by concubines.

With that she did the unthinkable and refused the request of the king. In his humiliation and drunkenness he banished Vashti forever. He would not be made a fool of in front of his councillors so feeling humiliated and angry, he set into motion a hasty, irrevocable and publicly decreed, regrettable decision. It was set into law and he could not call her back.

Without his queen, he was of course lonely and suggestions by his servants that they should seek out beautiful young virgins for the king to find another queen who would take the place of Vashti were put into place.

This might well have been the first "Miss Persia" pageant as a nationwide search began to find that special woman. This is where the story of Hadassah also known as Esther begins.

Hadassah was Esther's Jewish name which means "myrtle" a tree whose leaves only release their fragrance when crushed. It was a prophetic name for Esther as it turned out. It was her fragrance of character that was tested when her very life and the lives of her people were at stake. Esther also means "hidden" which is what her uncle advised her to do; to hide her true identity of being Jewish until the right time came to reveal it.

Esther agreed and went along with her uncle's warning. It is important to note that Esther was left an orphan by her parents and was raised by her uncle Mordecai and his wife.

Another interesting reference suggests that the names Esther and Mordecai may be related to stories about the Persian deities Ishtar and Marduk. Ishtar, a Babylonian goddess of love, means "a star". Marduk was the principle male god of Babylon. Some suggest that the similarities in the book of Esther were based on the older Babylonian story that the Jewish people heard during the Babylonian exile. Esther, a virgin was extraordinarily beautiful and was soon to be chosen as one of the candidates to be taken into the harem. It seemed that even the head eunuch, Hegai was pleased with her beauty and as a result, she found favour in his eyes. The preparation took twelve months until each candidate was considered acceptable for the king. In Cynthia Hillson Page's book "Esther's Days of Purification" she beautifully described an intensive and intentional beauty regime of purification that not only would seek the beautification of the body but of the soul and the spirit as well. It is well known that during the first six months she was prepared with oil of myrrh. As described previously, myrrh needs to be crushed for the benefits of the leaves to be of any medicinal or topical use and blended in perfumes and anointing oils.

We could spend pages discussing this first step of purification, but will only look at a few items. Throughout scripture, we see that oil of myrrh was given to Jesus on three occasions in his life on earth; at his birth, at his death on the cross and at his burial. So we can symbolically see that Esther was prepared for a "death to self". Esther would have to die to her own self-life, her own self-effort, her own ambitions, her own understanding and all that she once held dear in her life. As a result of giving up all she had, she also would be among those that would overcome. Other uses of the spice worth mentioning are that in biblical times, two bouquets of myrtle welcomed the Shabbat each week. Other Jewish celebrations and festivals used myrtle's fragrant branches symbolically: during Succoth-Feast of the Tabernacles as part of the lulav - four species; and Boughs of myrtle were worn by bridegrooms, used in the betrothal celebrations. It's delightful to know that Kate Middleton who married Prince William in 2011 included this famous plant in her bridal bouquet. The bouquet was filled with the traditional flowers of the Royal family including Myrtle, Lily of The Valley, Sweet

William, Hyacinth and Ivy. Each plant carried their own significant implication of what they symbolized to each family represented, both Royal and common.

Aromatherapy's usage of myrtle for skin care, respiratory ailments and the immune system is growing in today's health and wellness industry.

Esther's next months were filled by preparation with sweet odours. Perhaps, as mentioned in other portions of scripture, the odour was a sweet smell, acceptable and well pleasing to God. The baths of roses was symbolic of emotional healing, of cleansing of the mind, hurts and wounds from the past, washing over and healing with the waters of fragrant oils. It has been suggested that each candidate was given women as confidants and counsellors to help in the last stages of purifications, so that when each of them were presented to the king, they would be considered whole: body, spirit, mind and soul. Nothing was left to circumstance, but every part of the virgin's life was scrupulously examined. The future of the Queen depended on it as well as the Persian Empire.

"Esther was the Queen worthy of the best cosmetics. Hegai's overseeing of the chambers gave him constant access to the costly and pleasant herbs, flowers, spices, and resins found in ancient

Persia. The author and historian, Pliny the Elder, believes costly perfumes were made from saffron, roses and galbanum. These fragrances, all native to Persia, are believed to be the first perfumes.

Picture this: Esther is bathing and applying rose's oils, (unity, love and simplicity), lavender (dignity and excellence), frankincense (purity and worship), rosemary (remembrance), cinnamon (uprightness), saffron (mirth, great joy), galbanum (the choicest portion) and other spices, herbs, and floral essences. She is sipping herbal tea and eating special foods. She is being served by seven appointed maidens, who bring her into completion and perfection." [18]

Once she had been accepted and found in favour by King Ahasuerus, she was appointed Queen. The whole Persian Kingdom, its wealth and power was now at her disposal and nothing would be denied to her as Queen. More importantly to her and Mordecai, no one knew she was a Jew and that she and Mordecai were related.

"Esther was symbolic of the Jews who lived successfully in an alien culture. As a woman, she was not in a position of power, just as Diaspora Jews were not members of the power elite. As an orphan, she was separated from her parents, as Diaspora Jews were separated from their mother country.

With both these handicaps, she had to use every skill and advantage she had, as Diaspora Jews did. They, like Esther, had adapted themselves to their situation." [19]

It seems that very shortly after their marriage troubles started to quietly show up at their palace. The hatred of Haman, one of the King's highest officials, towards her uncle Mordecai who would not bow down to Haman, even though it is proper protocol, is fierce. Haman is outraged and indignant and a feud quietly starts between them and leads to a very dangerous plot to kill not only Mordecai but the destruction of the Jewish race in the one hundred and twenty seven nations that the king ruled over.

Can you image the fear that would grip your heart at the declaration of such a decree?? Mordecai, who is known by the king as he previously thwarted a plot on the king's life, yet the king does not know that he is Jewish. Even more so, Esther, the king's bride and queen is also a Jew. As Haman plots to kill the Jews, the king having agreed and the decree issued for every corner of his empire, Mordecai and Esther are faced with the thought of death.

Esther was deeply afraid, her life now was in danger as well as the lives of her people and it looked like there was nothing that she could do to prevent it.

Mordecai too was frantic and summoned Esther to
rise up then to be the heroin she was destined to
be. The appointed time of her favor and her
influence with the king was upon her when she
called the entire Jewish nation into fasting and
prayer for three days as she sought Jehovah's
guidance. Mordecai reminded her that this was her
appointed time and she was required to rise up
because she too was without protection from the
King. She humbly declared that even though she
had not been summoned by the King, she would
approach him, which could have resulted in her
immediate death, breaking the law as it were, while
inviting him to a banquet prepared just for him.
She once again found favor in his sight and
requested his and Haman's presence at a banquet
she had prepared just for them. Meanwhile Haman
was busy building gallows to hang Mordecai on, but
accepted and was delighted to be invited along with
the king to this very special occasion. King
Ahasuerus was charmed to once again be in her
presence and offered Esther anything she wanted
up to half of his kingdom. It is encouraging to see
that Esther had great influence on the King and
held out some hope for her as she again invited
them to a second banquet to which the King was in
agreement to attend. On that fateful night she
humbled herself before the King and plead for the
life of her people and herself. She revealed to the

King that the evil plot of Haman was actually against her and her Jewish people. Ultimately his Queen's pleas were acknowledged and she was given favour and pardon for them all as her petitions were granted.

It is hard to fathom the dictatorship of a King's rule as a sacral kingship. The absolute power of the king is foreign to us as we are accustomed to a democratic system of rule. To think that one could have unquestionable authority, whether good or bad seems incredulous. It was the sovereign act of God that saved the Jewish people through the handmaiden Esther. Her inner beauty of strength and grace, humility and concern was only magnified by her obedience. Her dedication to the assignment that God had given her, to love a pagan king, to even marry a foreigner is true obedience to the Lord Jehovah and to her uncle Mordecai. Without a doubt, it is evident that God used her to save His people and by His grace, a lasting legacy of Influence which is written in many books and sacred passages of the Bible.

DISCUSSION QUESTIONS:

What do you think Esther's biggest challenge was?

What would be yours?

Do you think that Mordecai should have submitted in bowing to Haman?

Do you think it might have averted the plot against the Jews?

What are some modern day Esther experiences you have had?

The Jewish people were all called to fast and pray for three days, have you ever felt a need to do the same in your own situation?

What do you think of the symbolism with fragrances, herbs, oils and spices?

Did you notice that in Jesus's life and death, herbs, spices and oils were used?

LISTENING TO GOD AND JOURNALING QUESTIONS?

Do you believe that Jesus has called you to be an Esther in your life? Ask Him when, where and what He's leading you through.

Have you ever faced a crisis moment where you wondered if God would come through? Maybe you are feeling like you are in the midst of a trial. What is Jesus saying to you?

Can you see where God wants to bathe you in precious oils and perfumes, and in the fragrance of His presence and word?

Do you see that you were meant to reign with Him and that like Esther you are the Queen in your Father's eye, a delight to Him??

Ask Him to show you what that looks like and how you can remain still while abiding in Him?

SCRIPTURES TO MEDIATE ON:

Proverbs 31:25 -26 She is clothed with strength and dignity

1 Peter 3:3-5 Gentle and quiet spirit

Psalm 37:30 Out of the mouth of a righteous woman

Ephesians 4: 15 Speak the truth in love

Psalm 84:11 Favour and honor bestowed

Philippians 3:14 Press on the race before you

SOMETHING TO THINK ABOUT:

"Do you know that we are created to sparkle with the light of God's creativity in us? When you are grateful that Jesus has made you preciously unique, you can't wait to hold your life up to reflect His light. You will dare to live out the beauty you were created to share with the world. Renewed and refined with the compassion of God."

Deborah Veuger

CHAPTER 8

A NEW DAY HAS COME

Now is the time for you to identify yourself as a daughter of the King, worthy of all of His gifts, promises, blessings, His unending and unfailing love, and grace He wants to give to you. Believing and walking in faith, it truly is a new day.

Understand that you are no longer a product of your past, as you are now a product of Christ's works on the cross - a new creation. You have the privilege of evaluating your past experiences in the light of who you are today.

You can now see that God longs for us to put our confidence in Him and not ourselves or others. To believe that "by faith", not by feelings, we can accept the full promises God has for us regarding His gift of being blessings, chosen and accepted.

My prayer for you as that as you listen for God to speak life and love into your own heart and mind that you will come away, whether you did this as a study group with friends, or on your own as a way of spending time with God, with the truth that Jesus loves you and nothing and no one can change that. His blood has bought your redemption and you are free to live the life He has destined you to have. One of my favorite sayings is "You go Girl" and that would be my advice for each of you.

Regardless of what the future holds, this one thing is for sure; God has already gone ahead of you and prepared the way. It may not always be easy, but He will be with you, and with that, you can go with confidence in the direction that He leads.

Jesus intended for you to have a wonderful life and journey with Him and when this life is over we will live with Him in Eternity for ever. It just doesn't get any better than that.

ENDNOTES

[1] Bar On, Bat-Ami. <u>Engendering Origins: Critical Feminist Readings in Plato and Aristotle</u>. State University of New York Press, New York, 1994.

[2] Gould, Carol C. <u>Beyond Domination: New Perspectives on Women and Philosophy</u>. Rowman & Allanheld, New Jersey, 1983.

Robinson, Charles Alexander Jr. <u>The Spring of Civilization.</u> EP Dutton and Company Inc., New York, 1954.

[3]Sealey, Raphael. <u>Women and Law in Classical Greece</u>. The University of North Carolina Press, Chapel Hill, 1990

[4] Donna Jordan and her husband Peter are founders of YWAM Associates International. Donna teaches extensively in conferences, churches, women´s retreats and Discipleship Training Schools around the world. The main focus of her teaching is that every Christian can

hear God´s voice and be led by His Spirit. Her study guides and DVD teachings on hearing God are available from the ministry. Used with permission

[5] Joseph Prince, <u>Blessed with Every Pneumatikos Blessing</u> Devotional, February 4, 2012

[6]Shaw, Nathan, <u>Spiritual Blessings in Heavenly Places</u>: The Heart of David Ministries, Prophetic Article, <u>http://www.heartofdavidministires.org//spiritual</u> blessing.html, 2006

[7] These are My Beloved Lyrics on http://www.lyricsmania.com/

From the album: Kari Jobe; released in February 10, 2009 by Integrity Music and Gateway Create Used by Permission

[8] Adapted from <u>The C.H. Spurgeon Collection</u>, Version 1 Volume 8, 1862 Sermon #471

[9]Oswald Chambers<u>, My Utmost for His Highest</u> devotional classic edition, Grand Rapids, Michigan: Copyrights 1935 by Dodd, Mead and Company, Inc.

[10]Philip Yancey, What's So Amazing About Grace? 1997 Zondervan, Grand Rapids, Michigan; p 70, p 280 Used by Permission of Zondervan. www.zondervan.com

[11]Piper, John, <u>Sealed by the Spirit to the Day of Redemption, Desiring God Foundation:</u> May, 1984 http://desiringgod.org/sermons/sealed -by-the-spirit-to-the..... Accessed December 19th, 2013

[12]Swindoll, Charles<u>, The Grace Awakening,</u> Nashville, TN: W Publishing Group, a division of Thomas Nelson, Inc., 1990, 1996, 2003 Used by Permission of Zondervan. www.zondervan.com

[13]Beaver, Pierce, <u>American Protestant Women in Mission</u>: Grand Rapids, MI., Eerdmans, 1982, p.135

[14] Pierson, Paul, <u>A Younger Church in Search of Maturity</u>: San Antonio, TX: Trinity University Press, 1974

[15]Neil T. Anderson, <u>Victory Over The Darkness Study Guide</u>, Bethany House Publishers, a division of Baker Publishing Group, 1994, 2000 "Used with Permission"

16Gerth, Holly, <u>You're Already Amazing</u>, Revell, a division of Baker Publishing Group, March 1, 2012 "Used by Permission"

[17]Meyers, Joyce, <u>God Is Not Mad at You</u>, FaithWords, Hatchette Book Group, New York, NY, September, 2013, Used by Permission

[18]Andrew, Gini, The Star and the Scepter, Grand Rapids, Michigan, US Zondervan Publishing Company, 1981

[19]Page, Cynthia, Esther's days of Purification, page 25, Precious Oils Up On the Hill (2010) https://preciousoils.wordpress.com/2010

[20]Fletcher, Elizabeth, Article on Esther, <u>www.womeninthebible.net/,Harper</u> Collins: Sydney Australia, 1997, accessed October 5, 2016

Made in the USA
Columbia, SC
18 February 2018